BASEBALL'S
Funniest People

BASEBALL'S
Funniest People

Michael J. Pellowski
Illustrated by Sanford Hoffman

Sterling Publishing Co., Inc.
New York

DEDICATION

To second baseman Morgan, shortstops
Melanie and Martin, and third baseman Matt . . .
the Pellowski All-Star team.

Library of Congress Cataloging-in-Publication Data

Pellowski, Michael.
    Baseball's funniest people / Michael J. Pellowski ; illustrated by
Sanford Hoffmann.
        p.   cm.
    Includes index.
    ISBN 0-8069-9442-8
    1. Baseball—Humor. 2. Baseball players—Quotations. 3. Baseball—
Anecdotes. I. Title.
GV873.P4   1997
796.357'0207—dc20   96-39060
                                                                CIP

            1   3   5   7   9   10   8   6   4   2

        Published by Sterling Publishing Company, Inc.
        387 Park Avenue South, New York, N.Y. 10016
                    © 1997 by Michael Pellowski
            Distributed in Canada by Sterling Publishing
        % Canadian Manda Group, One Atlantic Avenue, Suite 105
                Toronto, Ontario, Canada M6K 3E7
        Distributed in Great Britain and Europe by Cassell PLC
        Wellington House, 125 Strand, London WC2R 0BB, England
        Distributed in Australia by Capricorn Link (Australia) Pty Ltd.
    P.O. Box 6651, Baulkham Hills, Business Centre, NSW 2153, Australia
                Manufactured in the United States of America
                        All rights reserved

                Sterling ISBN 0-8069-9442-8

CONTENTS

INTRODUCTION

Baseball is a zany sport where practical jokes, goofy gags, and loony lines muttered by ballplayers are as much a part of the game as heroic home runs, dazzling no-hitters, and inspiring pep talks. Baseball jokesters range from fabled Hall of Famers and modern superstars to well-traveled reserves and lesser-known benchwarmers. Baseball history is crammed full of crazy coaches, oddball owners, and wacky players who have all contributed to the unforgettable mystique of America's favorite and sometimes outrageously funny sport. In the following pages, you will meet many of these characters and learn of their contributions to baseball folklore.

Michael J. Pellowski

BASEBALL'S WACKY ROSTER

CRANK CALLERS

Years ago, second baseman Ted Sizemore, a player for the Chicago Cubs, left a funny message on his phone answering machine. When anyone phoned Sizemore, this is the message the caller heard: "It's the bottom of the ninth. The bases are loaded. There are two outs and I'm up. Here's the pitch! There's a grounder to third! The throw is to first and . . . I'm out! That's right, I'm out!"

"E" FOR EFFORT

Shortstop Dave Concepcion of the Cincinnati Reds was known by the nickname "Elmer" during his playing days. How he got that nickname is a funny story. Concepcion was dubbed "Elmer" by rival shortstop Larry Bowa of the Philadelphia Phillies, a noted baseball jokester in his time. After a series of games during which Concepcion had difficulty making fielding plays, Larry walked up to Dave holding newspaper clippings of the Reds' box scores.

"Hey, Concepcion!" called Bowa. "Is your first name Elmer?" Before Concepcion could reply, Bowa showed him the box score clippings which read . . . E—Concepcion! Of course, the "E" stood for Error. Everyone had a good laugh at the gag and from that day on Dave Concepcion's nickname was "Elmer."

STEER CRAZY

Home-run slugger Ken Griffey of the Seattle Mariners and Team Manager Lou Piniella made a tasty little bet during batting practice in April of 1995. Griffey bet Piniella he could clout a certain number of balls out of the stadium in practice. The loser of the home run wager would have to buy the winner an expensive steak dinner. Lou accepted the bet and the contest was on. Unfortunately for Griffey, he lost and had to pay up. Equally unfortunate for Piniella, superstar Griffey's unique sense of humor played a part in paying off the

debt. Three days later, manager Lou Piniella walked into his office in the Mariners' clubhouse and discovered a 1,200-pound Hereford cow waiting for him. "There's your steak," Ken Griffey said to Lou Piniella.

OLD JOKE

Sometimes baseball players make honest replies to questions without realizing the humor in their responses. Take Hall-of-Famer Mel Ott, one of the game's greatest hitters. Young Mel was only sixteen years old when he was brought up to the Majors to play for the New York Giants. At the time, Ott was a catcher. New York's manager looked at the sixteen-year-old and asked him a question. "Son, did you ever play the outfield?" asked Manager John McGraw. Very seriously, Mel Ott replied, "Yes sir, when I was a kid."

CIRCUS PITCHMAN

Hulking relief pitcher Dick Radatz of the Boston Red Sox was known as the "Monster" during his playing days. However, as big as he was, Radatz wasn't without a sense of humor. One night Dick was visiting a circus when he spied the show's tall man—a guy who stood seven feet, seven inches high. Radatz eyed the giant with glee and remarked, "Man! What a strike zone!"

GRASS ROOTS

When the Philadelphia Phillies traveled to Houston, Texas, in July of 1966 to play in the Astrodome, some of the Phillies players were asked their opinions of the revolutionary new artificial turf. Philadelphia third baseman Dick Allen was later quoted as saying, "If cows don't eat it I ain't playing on it!"

FUNNY FIGHTING WORDS

Years later, when the six-foot, six-inch Dick Radatz was a member of the Montreal Expos, his team was involved in a bench-clearing brawl with the Pittsburgh Pirates. At that time, the Pirates had a shortstop named Fred Patek who stood five feet, six inches. As the opposing club members paired off to settle the dispute, Radatz looked at Patek and said, ''I'll take you and a player to be named later.''

HARE-BRAINED

Hall-of-Fame baseball star Walter James Vincent Maranville is better known by his funny nickname, which is Rabbit. Rabbit Maranville played for the Boston Braves in the mid-1900s. Maranville was one of baseball's earliest pranksters. Once when it was his turn to bat, he crawled through umpire Hank O'Day's legs on his way to home plate—much to the delight of the hometown crowd!

HOMEWARD BOUND

Pitcher Pat Caraway of the Chicago White Sox pulled off a zany stunt in his rookie season in the major leagues. Caraway, who was a native Texan, found it tough to endure the bitter cold of early-season games played in blustery Chicago. He complained and complained and complained. Finally, the manager of the team, tired of hearing Pat grumble about the chilly weather, asked, "What do you want me to do about the weather?"

"Well," replied Caraway, "can I at least go home and get an overcoat?"

"Fine! Go get an overcoat," the manager shouted. And so Pat Caraway exited the stadium, left Chicago, and flew home to Texas to get an overcoat.

SHOE THING

Fresco Thompson, who became Vice President of the old Brooklyn Dodgers, was one of baseball's great funny men. His wit was even quicker than his bat. Fresco, who for a while played alongside hilarious Babe Herman in the outfield for the Dodgers, once described Herman's lack of fielding ability this way: "Babe wore a glove for only one reason. It was a league custom." In his later years as a member of the New York Giants, Thompson played for manager Bill Terry and was seldom used. Fresco spent most of his days with the Giants relaxing on the bench in the dugout. One afternoon, he was shocked to hear Bill Terry call for him to go into a game as a pinch runner. Fresco Thompson yawned, stretched, and refused to play by saying, "I'd love to Bill, but I just had my shoes shined!"

THE ANSWER MAN

When Fresco Thompson was a member of the daffy Dodgers managed by Wilbert Robinson, Thompson shared a locker with Babe Herman, a super hitter but an inept fielder at best. Babe didn't like sharing his locker with Fresco and made his feelings public. "I don't like dressing with a .250 hitter," Herman announced.

Without a moment's hesitation, Fresco yelled out, "And I don't like dressing with a .250 fielder!"

UDDER NONSENSE

Cincinnati Reds' hurler Norm Charlton had his hands full when the Reds played the Atlanta Braves on August 5, 1989. In fact, Norm was the key player in a successful squeeze play which delayed the start of the Reds–Braves contest at Riverfront Stadium. A herd of cows was ushered out onto the playing field before the game, and a milking contest was held as part of Cincinnati's Farmers' Night festivities. Norm Charlton won the milking contest, but the Braves won the baseball game that followed the udder nonsense.

SUITS ME

In 1903, Ed Pinnance was one of the first Native Americans to play Major League baseball. Ed was a solid player with a fondness for a strange piece of luggage. When he showed up at the Philadelphia Athletics' training camp, he was carrying a suitcase hand-made from the hide of an elk he'd shot with a bow and arrow.

SMART MOUTH

Outfielders Reggie Jackson and Mickey Rivers were teammates on the 1977 New York Yankees team. Once during a ride on the team bus, Jackson, who was known to be slightly egotistical, started to swap insults with Rivers in a good-natured way. Reggie called Mickey "dumb" and claimed that he himself was much smarter. "I have an IQ of 160," boasted Reggie Jackson.

"Oh, yeah," retorted a sly Mickey Rivers. "You can't even spell IQ!"

NAME GAME

After Mickey Rivers retired as a player, he got a job working with the New York Yankees and manager Billy Martin as a special assistant. One day during spring training, Rivers went into Martin's office and told him he wanted to be known from that day on as "Miguel Rivera" instead of Mickey Rivers.

"What's wrong with the name Mickey Rivers?" manager Martin wanted to know.

"Too many people are looking for me," zany Mickey Rivers replied very seriously.

BIRD BRAIN

Joe "Ducky" Medwick was a great player for the St. Louis Cardinals. He also had a wacky sense of humor. During his prime, Medwick visited Vatican City in Rome with a group of famous entertainers. The group was granted an audience with the Pope. Members of the group were introduced to the Pope one by one and announced their occupations. "I'm a singer," said the first member of the group.

"I'm a comic," said the next person to be introduced.

When it was Medwick's turn to meet the Pope, Ducky said, "Your Holiness, I'm a Cardinal."

THE HOLE STORY

In 1993, ex-Phillies infielder Dave Sveum was talking about his former team and said he missed playing in the City of Brotherly Love about as much as he missed having a hole in his head. When Philadelphia General Manager Lee Thomas heard about Sveum's comment, he fired off a fast retort which rates as one of baseball's funniest replies. "Dave Sveum is a real classy guy," he said. "We did give him an opportunity—a big opportunity. He says he misses playing here like a hole in the head. Well, what about the hole in his bat?"

BULL PENNED

Pitcher Moe Drabowsky, who played for the St. Louis Cardinals during the early 1970s, had a wacky way of passing time, while out in the bullpen. While games were in progress, he often used the bullpen telephone to order a pizza. Once he even called the opposing team's bullpen, disguised his voice, and ordered an opposing pitcher to warm up.

BATTY HUMOR

First baseman John Kruk of the Philadelphia Phillies had a quick bat when he was playing in the Major Leagues and an even quicker wit when he retired from baseball in 1995. After Kruk singled in a game on July 20, 1995, he immediately quit the game of baseball so he could end his 10-year career with a hit. After leaving professional baseball, Kruk was interviewed on late-night television by comedian David Letterman. When asked about the rigorous routine of his retirement, John Kruk replied, "I get up early every morning and lie on the couch."

SIZE WISE

Huge Ted Kluszewski played for the California Angels in 1961. Kluszewski, who stood six feet, two inches tall and had massive, bulging biceps, was given a new roommate that season by manager Bill Rigney. Big Klu's roomie was Albie Pearson, a great player who stood only five feet, five inches tall. When Kluszewski first laid eyes on his new roomie, he told Pearson, "I get the bed in our room. You get the dresser drawer." Albie Pearson laughed at Kluszewski's joke. One night later that season, Kluszewski came into his room to find Pearson sound asleep in bed. Big Ted lifted Albie out of the bed without waking him and positioned Pearson's dozing form in an open dresser drawer. And that's where Albie Pearson was when he woke up.

SHORT STORY

Albie Pearson stood tall at the plate when it came to hitting, but he took a lot of kidding about his size. Someone once said of Albie, "If he walked around with a lit cigar in his mouth he'd burn everyone in the knee."

Another teammate of Albie's had this to say: "Having a catch with Albie Pearson is very relaxing. It's like throwing downhill."

NUTTY NEWS

Sportswriter Edward T. Murphy was a baseball fan with an ironic sense of humor. Trying to think positive during the 1930s, when the Brooklyn Dodgers fielded some mighty weak squads, Murphy wrote, "Overconfidence may cost the Dodgers sixth place."

GEORGE THE JESTER

George Steinbrenner, the owner of the New York Yankees baseball club, is a man known for making tough and sometimes even harsh business decisions when it comes to handling his beloved ball club. Steinbrenner is more famous for firing managers and coaches than he is for firing off one-liners and jokes. However, at the start of the 1996 American League season, George proved he could jest with the best.

When the Yankees visited Texas in early April of 1996 to play the Texas Rangers, one of the television broadcasters covering the game was retired second baseman Joe Morgan. During the broadcast George Steinbrenner commanded Yankee media relations director Rick Cerrone to deliver a prank message to Hall-of-Famer Morgan. Steinbrenner's note to Joe Morgan read: "Please contact me tomorrow at Yankee Stadium regarding a comeback at second base . . . we are wide open." George's gag offer made everyone in the press box laugh, including Morgan, a happily retired ex-second baseman.

PIE-EYED

Larry Anderson was the team clown of the 1993 Phila-delphia Phillies. Anderson, who liked to pester his team-mates with wacky questions like "Why do people sing *Take Me Out to the Ballgame* at the stadium when they're already there?" and "Why do people drive on the park-

way and park in the driveway?," got a bitter taste of his own nutty medicine in April of 1993. While Anderson was taping an important television interview, teammates Curt Schilling and Pete Incaviglia sneaked up behind him and smacked him in the face with a shaving-cream pie. Larry Anderson's pie-in-the-eye television interview turned into an instant smash hit thanks to the practical joke.

SAY, WHAT?

Manager Lefty Phillips, who was the skipper of the California Angels in 1969, could rival baseball's best when it came to bizarre double-talk. Talking about the lack of output from his star players, Phillips once said, "Our phenoms ain't phenomenating." On another occasion, Lefty was asked about a tough loss his Angels' squad had just suffered and commented, "It's all water under the dam."

GRIMM HUMOR

Manager Charlie Grimm led the Chicago Cubs to National League pennants in 1932 and 1935, but both of his squads fizzled in World Series play. In 1932, he lost to manager Joe McCarthy's New York Yankees team four games to none, and in 1935 he was defeated by Manager Mickey Cochrane's Detroit Tigers team four games to two. Nevertheless, Charlie Grimm had a world championship sense of humor. Once a scout called him up to brag about a young pitcher he'd discovered. "The kid is great," insisted the scout. "He struck out 27 batters in one game. No one even hit a foul ball off of him until the ninth inning."

Grimm paused to reflect on the report and then replied, "Sign the kid who hit the foul ball. We need hitters more than pitchers."

METAL PLATES

The first baseball game in Berlin, Germany, was played in June of 1912, and the wackiest guy on the field that day was the home-plate umpire. No one knows his name, but they know what he wore to call balls and strikes that day. It was a suit of armor!

LET'S SEE

There is more than one way to get an umpire's goat. Skipper Charlie Grimm didn't always argue with the men in blue to make his point. Once umpire Charlie Moran (who had been a college football coach before his umpiring days) made a bad call against Grimm's Chicago Cubs team. As angry players rushed out to fight with umpire Moran, Charlie Grimm got between his players and the ump. Charlie raised his hands to calm down his angry squad and stated, "The first person to lay a finger on this blind old man will be fined fifty bucks!"

SICK HUMOR

Seattle Mariners superslugger Jay Buhner is a fun-loving player with a hot temper and a sick sense of humor. Buhner, who clouted 20 or more home runs per season from 1990 to 1995, can't stomach failure. Once while playing golf with some Seattle teammates, he missed a shot and threw his club in disgust. When that display didn't cool his temper, he tried to toss his entire golf bag but found it tightly fastened to his motorized cart. Since Jay couldn't undo the bag from the cart and throw it, he did the next best thing. He flipped over the entire golf cart.

On the field, Jay Buhner's sick sense of humor can be upsetting to those who witness his most famous prank. Buhner can force himself to vomit at will. Jay calls his sick stunt "blurping" and explains it as a combination of burping and vomiting. Buhner usually "blurps" to nauseate rookie players. However, Jay Buhner once pulled his "blurping" gag in the outfield, which caused fellow Mariners outfielders Ken Griffey and Kevin Mitchell to become sick to their stomachs. In a yucky display of team unity, all three players threw up in the outfield during the game.

INSIGHT

Paul Casanova, a catcher for the old Washington Senators during the 1960s, had a bad habit of dropping pop-ups. When someone asked him if he planned to make improvements in that area, he was ready with a witty reply. "This year I have a new strategy," Casanova said. "I am not going to close my eyes when I try to catch pop-ups."

TALKING BASEBALL

Pitcher Mark Fidrych of the Detroit Tigers was a colorful character during his playing days. While standing on the mound, Fidrych would talk directly to the baseball he held in his hand. On other occasions, if one of his infielders made a good fielding play, Mark would storm off the mound and offer the appropriate player a vigorous congratulatory handshake before continuing to pitch in the game.

CLOWN PRINCES OF BASEBALL

LARRY "YOGI" BERRA

Hall-of-Famer Larry "Yogi" Berra, who played for the New York Yankees and managed the Yankees and the New York Mets, was not only one of the game's greatest hitting catchers, but also one of baseball's funniest guys. His wacky remarks, side-splitting stories, and nutty exploits are definitely of funny Hall-of-Fame caliber.

It's a Repeat

When it comes to understated daffiness, Yogi is in a class by himself. He once remarked, "It's déjà vu all over again."

Car Trouble

One evening, Yogi Berra was driving to a banquet with Yankee teammate Phil Rizzuto. "Yogi, we're lost," groaned Rizzuto.

"Yeah," agreed Berra, "but we're making good time."

Fenced In

On another occasion, a reporter asked Yogi how things were going for him. Berra replied, "I'm straddling the other side of the fence right now."

Food for Thought

When one of Yogi's favorite restaurants started to attract too many customers, Berra stopped patronizing it. When someone asked him about the restaurant, Yogi said, "Nobody goes there anymore. It's too crowded."

A Swinging Guy

Yogi Berra was famous for swinging at and usually hitting pitches out of the strike zone. However, on one occasion he swung at a terrible pitch way out of the zone and struck out. "Humph," Berry grumbled on his way back to the dugout. "How can a pitcher that wild stay in the league?"

Eye Sore

Yogi was at spring training in Florida one summer when something weird happened during a rain delay. Two streakers jumped over the centerfield fence and ran buck naked across the infield. When Berra went home that night, his wife asked him about the incident. "Were the streakers boys or girls?" she asked Yogi.

"I don't know," he replied. "They had bags over their heads."

Fan Support

When Yogi Berra visited his hometown of St. Louis in 1947 as a member of the New York Yankees, the fans there staged a celebration in his honor. After he was presented with numerous gifts and mementoes, Yogi walked up to a microphone to make a speech. Berra took a deep breath and said, "I want to thank all of you fans for making this night necessary."

Wrong Turn

People seldom ask Yogi Berra for directions. Yogi once said, "When you come to a fork in the road, take it!"

Timely Remark

When Yogi Berra showed up late for an important meeting, he quickly came up with what he thought was a good excuse for his tardiness. "But this is the earliest I've ever been late," he said.

Huh?

Yogi had this to say about league MVP (Most Valuable Player) Frank Robinson's hitting style: "If you can't copy him, don't imitate him."

Tock to Me

A teammate once asked Yogi Berra a simple question. "What time is it?" the guy asked.

Yogi looked at him and answered, "You mean right now?"

Home Boy

When Yogi Berra was the manager of the New York Yankees, he was interviewed at the start of the season. "I love home openers," Yogi said, "whether they're at home or on the road."

Crazy Qualifications

When Yogi Berra was named manager of the New York Yankees in 1964, he was asked what qualified him for the position. Said Yogi, "You observe a lot by watching."

Music Man

In 1964, the New York Yankees managed by Yogi Berra suffered though a difficult losing season. After one really disheartening loss, Berra boarded the team bus and was shocked to hear utility infielder Phil Linz playing happy tunes on his harmonica. Upset by the team's defeat, Berra got into a loud argument with Linz and ended up fining him two hundred dollars for playing the harmonica. The next year when Phil Linz signed his Yankee contract, he got a raise in salary which included a two-hundred-dollar bonus. With the bonus was a letter from Yogi telling Linz to spend the two hundred dollars on harmonica lessons!

Crowd Control

Sportscaster Joe Garagiola was talking baseball with his buddy Yogi Berra. The topic turned to the Kansas City Athletics, a team that at the time was having problems drawing fans to its games.

"The Athletics can't seem to draw a good crowd at home," Garagiola said.

Yogi agreed. "If the fans don't want to come out," Berra said, "nobody can stop them."

Handy Guy

Once Yogi was discussing his teammate Mickey Mantle. "He can hit just as good right-handed as he can left-handed," said Yogi. "He's just naturally amphibious."

Light Humor

Yogi Berra was playing in a World Series game on an October afternoon when the sinking sun cast a dark shadow across the playing field. Looking out across the diamond, Yogi commented, "Gee, it gets late early out there."

Don't Make Waves

One afternoon in the New York locker room, Yogi Berra was telling some rookie players about his first days with the Yankees. Listening as he worked was Pete Sheehy, the clubhouse man. "I was in the Navy the first time I came in here," Yogi said as he pointed at the clubhouse floor. "In fact, I had on my sailor uniform," Berra added. Then he turned to speak to Pete Sheehy. "I bet you thought I didn't look like much of a ballplayer the first time you saw me, huh Pete?"

Pete Sheehy laughed and answered. "You didn't even look like much of a sailor."

A Swinging Guy

In 1982, the New York Yankees managed by Yogi Berra had difficulty hitting home runs. In fact, during one stretch of 28 games the Yankee club clouted a total of only 14 home runs. Explaining his team's lack of power at the plate to the press, Yogi Berra said, "We're swinging at too many bad balls; that's why we're not hitting home runs."

When a reporter on hand mentioned that Yogi himself was notorious for swinging at bad balls during his playing career, Yogi was quick to respond. "Yeah," snapped Berra, "but I hit 'em!"

Class Act

Yogi tells a story about his days in school. He said he once took a test and answered every question wrong. The teacher called him up to her desk and said, "Lawrence, I don't believe you know anything."

Lawrence "Yogi" Berra looked at his teacher and replied, "Ma'am, I don't even suspect anything."

Some Traveling Music

While playing on the road one year, Yankee outfielder Mickey Mantle looked at Yogi Berra's suitcases and shook his head in dismay. Berra's suitcases were battered and worn. "Yogi," said Mantle, "why don't you buy yourself some new luggage?"

"Why should I buy new luggage?" Yogi snapped. "I only use it for traveling."

JAY HANNA DEAN

Jay Hanna Dean (who sometimes called himself Jerome Herman Dean) more than lived up to the nutty nickname "Dizzy" given to him by an Army sergeant while

Dean was serving in the Armed Forces. Dizzy Dean was an All-Star pitcher for the famous St. Louis Cardinals team known as the "Gas House Gang." The Gang included other zany baseball stars like John "Pepper" Martin, Leo "The Lip" Durocher, and Frankie Frisch. When it comes to ranking baseball's all-time wackiest and funniest person, Dizzy Dean's name just might get top billing.

Name Game

In 1934, pitcher Dizzy Dean won 30 games for the St. Louis Cardinals and lost only 7 games. Dean figured he was due a hefty raise, so he went to see General Manager Branch Rickey. "I want a twenty-thousand-dollar raise," Dizzy said.

Branch Rickey almost fainted. "Judas Priest! You're not worth that kind of money," Rickey shouted.

Dizzy looked Branch in the eye and replied, "I don't know who Judas Priest is. My name's Dean and I'm worth every penny of it."

Punny Position

Dizzy Dean was a great pitcher, but he often had trouble retiring New York Giants slugger Bill Terry. In one game where Dean was matched against Terry, Bill smashed a liner off Dizzy's leg his first time up. The next time he was up, Bill Terry cracked a liner that sizzled past Dizzy's head. On his third trip to the plate, Terry rocked one off Dizzy Dean's glove for a hit. Finally Pepper Martin called time out and walked to the mound from his position at third base. "Hey, Diz," said Pepper, "I don't think you're playing him deep enough."

Yo! Brother

In 1934, Dizzy's brother Paul "Daffy" Dean was also a member of the St. Louis Cardinals pitching staff. In September of that year, the Dean brothers were scheduled to appear on the mound in a doubleheader against the Brooklyn Dodgers. Dizzy Dean pitched the first game of the doubleheader. Going into the eighth inning, Dizzy was hurling a no-hitter. However, in the last two innings Dizzy gave up three hits but still easily won the game.

Daffy Dean took the mound for the second game and turned in a dazzling pitching performance. He bested his brother's three-hitter by hurling a no-hitter for the win. After the second game ended, Dizzy ran out to congratulate Daffy. As the brothers shook hands, Dizzy asked, "Why didn't you tell me you were going to pitch a no-hitter? Then I would have pitched one too!"

A Bit Hit

One day the St. Louis Gas House Gang took on an opposing team that had a weak pitching staff. After four straight St. Louis players were issued walks, the starting pitcher was yanked from the game. The next pitcher walked two more Cardinals players and hit the next two batters with pitched balls. The ninth batter in the order, pitcher Dizzy Dean, then stepped up to the plate. Dean swung at the first pitch and dribbled the ball back to the mound. The opposing hurler had trouble fielding the ball and Diz was safe at first. "A fine team I'm playing on," said Dizzy to the first base coach. "It isn't enough that I do the pitching, I have to do the hitting, too."

News Flash

On one occasion, Dizzy Dean was batting when he was hit in the head by a pitched ball. Dean was rushed to a hospital. Baseball fans anxious for medical news about the status of the St. Louis star cheered and laughed when a press report stated that Dizzy Dean's head was X-rayed and the test revealed nothing!

Teacher's Pest

After Dizzy Dean's playing days ended due to an injury, he became a famous baseball broadcaster on radio. However, Dean was a simple farm boy who had a lively imagination but a limited education. More often than not he mispronounced words and used incorrect grammar. One day, he was confronted by a schoolteacher who proceeded to scold him on the way he butchered language. "How can a network allow you to appear in front of a microphone when you don't even know the King's English?" she snapped.

"But, Ma'am," answered Dizzy Dean, "I do know it. In fact, I also know that the Queen is English."

Weather Vain

While broadcasting a baseball game on the radio which was held up by a thunderstorm, Dizzy had this to say to his listeners: "If you don't know why the game is being delayed," said Dean, "stick your head out of an open window."

Well, Excuse Me

On another occasion, Dizzy Dean had the misfortune of loudly belching during a radio broadcast. He quickly excused himself and explained to his startled listeners, "It's okay because I excused myself, so let's get back to the game."

CHARLES FINLEY

"I don't want to be remembered as a kook," Charlie Finley said, "but as an owner who did his best to make the game better." In a way, Charles O. Finley got his wish. He is the man mainly responsible for the designated hitter rule which is in use in Major League baseball's American League. However, Charles Finley will also be remembered as one of baseball's wackiest club owners.

The Merry Mascots

In the 1960s, Charles O. Finley was the owner of the Kansas City Athletics. One day, he decided the team might play better if it had a mascot. The mascot Mr. Finley decided on for his Kansas City squad was a mule, which Finley called "Charlie O.," naming it after himself. He also let the mule graze in the stadium's outfield.

Charlie came up with another wild animal idea shortly thereafter. Behind the outfield in the Athletics' home stadium was a hill covered with pasture land. Charlie put a sheep out in that pasture and dyed its wool green and gold—the team colors of the Kansas City Athletics.

Stump the Umps

Boring baseball tasks like resupplying the home-plate umpire with baseballs were given a hilarious twist in the Athletics' home stadium. Team owner Charlie Finley had baseballs delivered to the plate umpire by a mechanical rabbit that popped out of the ground!

The umpires were also given a treat during the fifth inning of every home game thanks to Mr. Finley. Finley had water and cookies delivered to the umps. In fact, the cookies were made by an A's employee named Debbie Fields who later established her own cookie business. Mrs. Fields' baked goods are now very famous.

Think Fast

In the mid-1960s, Charles Finley realized Major League baseball games sometimes proceed too slowly for the fans. Charlie came up with several ideas on speeding up the game which he pitched to baseball Commissioner Ford Frick. Finley wanted the rules of the game changed so that a batter would be issued a walk if the pitcher threw only three balls instead of four. He also wanted a 30-second time limit between a hurler's pitches. His wacky ideas were never given serious consideration.

Colorful

Baseballs have always been white. If Charlie Finley had gotten his way, that would not be so. Charlie once tried to have the game of baseball played with orange balls. He even started a company which produced orange baseballs.

What a Pitchman

Mr. Charles O. Finley had a soft spot in his heart (others said he had a soft spot in his head) for pitchers. In 1965, he signed one of the game's greatest hurlers to pitch for the Athletics. That pitcher was the immortal Satchell Paige. However, Paige was nearly 60 years old at the time, and Finley signed him to pitch just one game.

When Charlie signed pitcher Jim Hunter to a contract, he decided Hunter needed a nickname. Mr. Charlie O. Finley loved baseball nicknames. Charlie asked Jim what he liked to do when he wasn't playing baseball. "I like to go fishing for catfish," answered Jim.

"From now on you'll be Catfish Hunter," Charlie Finley announced. To this day, the nickname "Catfish" has stuck with Jim Hunter.

Charlie Finley tried to tag a new name on another of his famous hurlers, Vida Blue, an All-Star pitcher and a Cy Young Award winner. Finley tried talking his young superstar into changing his first name from Vida to "True" so he would be known as "True Blue." Vida Blue absolutely refused, and he kept his first name despite the protests of wacky Charles O. Finley.

Clubhouse Rap

The Kansas City Athletics moved west and became the Oakland Athletics in 1968. Charles Finley was never one to stand in the way of progress. He was also an owner who believed in keeping his players entertained. In fact, a batboy for the A's named Stanley Burrell was encouraged to dance in the clubhouse to entertain Charlie's players. That dancing batboy later became rap music mega-star M.C. Hammer.

FLOYD "BABE" HERMAN

When Floyd Herman came to the Major Leagues, he brought along his own special bats. Ty Cobb looked at the lumber and remarked that the bats were heavier than the ones used by Babe Ruth. Herman turned to Cobb and said, "I figure if I use heavier wood I'll hit the ball farther than Ruth." Soon after that boast, players began calling Floyd "Babe Herman."

Thoughtless

Babe Herman was a great hitter for the old Brooklyn Dodgers. However, Babe resented the fact that he was sometimes referred to as a talented, but goofy, player. "I'm a smart fella," Babe once told a reporter. "I read a lot of books. Go ahead. Ask me a question about anything."

The reporter thought for a minute. Finally he said to Babe, "What do you think of the Napoleonic Era?"

"Ha!" scoffed Babe Herman, "it should have been scored a hit!"

Ah, Skip It

Babe Herman's wacky ways are legendary. Babe didn't like to report to spring training, so he seldom signed his yearly contract until the season was about to begin. Everyone thought Babe "held out" each year just to squeeze more money out of the Dodgers team, which might not have been the whole truth. A teammate once asked Babe, "Is it worth skipping spring training every year just to get a few more dollars?"

Wacky Babe Herman, the worst fielder in baseball, replied, "I don't do it for the money. The longer I stay out of training camp the less chance I have of getting hit by a fly ball."

Smoke Screen

On another occasion, Babe Herman cornered several reporters in the Dodgers' locker room after a game and tried to convince them there was nothing nutty about his behavior. After a long talk, he finished by stating, ''I'm just a normal guy.'' He then pulled a cigar out of his jacket pocket and began to puff on it. Babe didn't have to light the cigar. The stogie was lit the entire time it was in his pocket!

Welcome Response

One sizzling hot summer day, Babe Herman showed up at the ballpark wearing a silk suit. "Mr. Herman, you look so cool," a female fan said to him.

"Thank you, Ma'am," replied Babe Herman. "You don't look so hot yourself."

All Hail Babe Herman

The stories about Babe Herman's blunders in the outfield are endless. Babe was a terrible fielder, but such a terrific hitter that he was one of manager Wilbert Robinson's favorite players. In fact, in Wilbert's eyes Babe could do no wrong. That sometimes irked other Dodger players, including pitcher Hollis Thurston and backup catcher Paul Richards.

One afternoon, the Dodgers were beating the Chicago Cubs when Chicago pitcher Kiki Cuyler stepped to the plate. As Thurston and Richards watched from the Dodgers bullpen in right field, Cuyler swung and lofted an easy fly ball down the right-field foul line. The right fielder should have caught it . . . but the right fielder was Babe Herman! Babe never saw the ball. In fact, he never moved until the ball hit the turf just inside the foul line. By the time Babe threw the ball in, Cuyler was standing on third base with a lucky triple.

When the inning ended, Hollis Thurston said to Paul Richards, "Let's walk to the bench and hear what Robinson says to Herman about the fly ball." The men were sure Babe was going to get bawled out.

When manager Wilbert Robinson saw Thurston and Richards approaching, he stepped out of the dugout and scowled at them. "Hey, you two!" he hollered. "What were you doing in the bullpen, sleeping? Why didn't you yell to Babe that Cuyler's hit was going to be a fair ball?"

Triple Trouble

Could Babe Herman hit! However, he didn't always think straight. One day the daffy outfielder came to the plate with the bases loaded and no outs. He quickly walloped a triple. Unfortunately for Babe and the Dodgers, the triple turned into a double play when Herman raced past two of his Brooklyn teammates on the base paths in his rush to reach third base. The runners he passed were declared out.

Bonk

Babe Herman was a terrible fielder who muffed count-less catches of fly balls in the outfield. Still, he always tried to convince reporters he wasn't that bad a fielder. "If a fly ball ever hits me on the head, I'll quit the game of baseball forever," Babe promised.

"What if one hits you on the shoulder?" a reporter asked Babe.

"The shoulder?" replied Babe Herman. "That doesn't count."

Don't Bet on Babe

Wilbert Robinson was the manager of a daffy Dodgers team that included Casey Stengel, Babe Herman, and Fresco Thompson. One afternoon Robinson and Her-man were sitting in a hotel lobby when a former friend of Wilbert's walked by. The man had lost all of his investments in the stock market crash during World War I. "That poor guy lost all his money during the war," Wilbert Robinson explained to Babe Herman.

Babe scratched his head in a puzzled fashion. "You mean he bet on the Germans?" Babe asked.

Bogus Babe

During his heyday, Babe Herman was a well-known ce-lebrity. However, for a short period of time an imposter made the rounds of New York restaurants and night-clubs claiming to be Babe. "Look," Babe Herman said to the press when asked about the imposter. "Showing up that fake is easy. Just take the guy out and hit him a fly ball. If the bum catches it, you know it ain't the real Babe Herman!"

HERMAN "GERMANY" OR "DUTCH" SCHAEFER

Herman "Germany" Schaefer played Major League baseball from 1901 to 1918. He was a member of the Washington Senators, the Chicago Cubs, the Detroit Tigers, and the Cleveland Indians. At the time of World War I, when Germany as a country wasn't too popular, Herman Schaefer dropped his original nickname and called himself "Dutch" instead. No matter what name you call him, Germany Schaefer was one of the game's craziest clowns.

Hit or Be Missed

When Schaefer was playing second base for the Detroit Tigers, he entered the game as a pinch hitter. Since Germany wasn't known for his skill as a batter, the crowd booed. Schaefer turned toward the crowd and doffed his cap. "Ladies and gentlemen," he announced, "permit me to present Herman Schaefer, the world's greatest batsman. I will now demonstrate my hitting prowess."

Amazingly, Germany stepped up to the plate and clouted the next pitch for a home run. Germany raced down the line and slid into first base. He stood up and yelled, "At the quarter Schaefer leads by a head!" He then dashed toward second and slid into the base. He got up and shouted, "At the half, the great Herman Schaefer leads by a length." He ran and slid into third base. Germany jumped up. "Schaefer leads by a mile!" he yelled out as he ran for home. He slid into the plate and stood up. Germany Schaefer turned toward the crowd and made an announcement. "This concludes Herman Schaefer's afternoon performance," he bellowed. "The world's greatest batsman thanks you, one and all." He then trotted off the field.

Put It in Reverse

One of Germany Schaefer's wackiest baseball stunts occurred when he was a member of the Washington Senators. It all began with the Senators' Clyde Milan on third and Schaefer on first. Germany wanted to draw a throw from the opposing catcher so Milan could score. When the pitcher delivered the ball to the plate, Schaefer slowly started to second. When the catcher refused to throw the ball, Germany Schaefer didn't like being ignored by the opposing catcher. The zany

Schaefer was determined to make the catcher throw the ball. On the next pitch Germany Schaefer pulled a reverse steal. He left second base and ran back to first. The catcher still didn't throw and Schaefer was safe again. His feat went down in baseball history as one of the silliest steals ever. Soon after Germany Schaefer's wacky steal, a rule was passed making a reverse steal illegal.

Well, Excuse Me!

On another occasion, Germany Schaefer tried to steal home. He slid into the plate in a cloud of dust and was called out by the umpire. "Didn't I knock the ball out of the catcher's hands?" Germany asked the umpire.

"Nope," answered the ump.

"Didn't I get here before the ball?" he argued.

"No!" barked the umpire.

"Didn't the catcher miss the tag?" Schaefer asked.

"He got you," the umpire yelled.

An angry Germany Schaefer threw down his cap in disgust. He then turned toward the grandstand and hollered to the crowd, "Ladies and gentlemen, I've run out of excuses!"

JOE GARAGIOLA

Joe Garagiola may not have been one of the game's greatest catchers, but he is one of baseball's best storytellers.

Ho! Ho! Hotel!

Garagiola tells a tall tale about a not-too-bright catcher who was fined by his manager for breaking training rules. "Don't try to fool me," the manager told his player. "I know your tricks. And I know all about that hotel episode in San Francisco."

The catcher scratched his head and seemed puzzled. "But skipper," he said, "you've got me mixed up with someone else. I never stayed in no Hotel Episode in San Francisco."

Family Fun

Someone asked catcher Joe Garagiola what Hall-of-Famer Stan Musial was really like. "Stan was a nice guy," Garagiola said. "Whenever I caught against him he'd step up to the plate and ask me about my family." Joe smiled and then continued, "But before I could answer he'd be on third base!"

Dough Boy

After his Major League career ended, Joe Garagiola worked as a broadcaster of major league games. He remembers the early days when the hapless New York Mets had difficulty winning games. During that period he attended a banquet in New York City. When a waiter laid a basket of breadsticks on his table, Garagiola quipped, "I see the Mets' bats have arrived."

Strike Breaker

When catcher Joe Garagiola was a member of the Pittsburgh Pirates, he faced fireballer Robin Roberts. After a Pirate batter clubbed a triple, Roberts heated up his fastball for the next three Pirate batters. He wiffed the first one on five pitches. Then Joe Garagiola stepped up to the plate and Robin Roberts struck him out on three pitches. "Doggone," Garagiola complained. "That was embarrassing. He could have at least worked on me a little."

Can't Resist

Sports broadcaster Joe Garagiola tells the story of Smead Jolley, a great fastball hitter. Jolley is up at the plate with runners on first and third. The guy on first breaks from the base to steal second. The catcher throws to second. The guy on third sees the throw and starts to run home. The shortstop cuts off the throw to second and fires a perfect strike to the plate. It's going to be a close play at home. At the plate, Smead Jolley watches intently. When the hard throw from the shortstop comes across the plate, Smead Jolley swings and cracks the ball into the outfield. "Hey," the home-plate ump yells to Jolley, "what are you doing?"

"Sorry, ump," answers Smead. "I couldn't resist. That's the first fastball I've seen in weeks."

Swan Song

Quick-witted commentator Joe Garagiola talks about a baseball team that was so bad that they had five runs scored against them during the National Anthem.

BASEBALL'S CRAZY CLUBHOUSE

PLANE CRAZY

All-Star pitcher Don Drysdale, of the Los Angeles Dodgers, fired off almost as many funny lines as he did fastballs during his playing career. Once after the Dodgers' team plane was forced to make an emergency landing, Drysdale explained the situation by saying, "There wasn't much of a delay. We only had to change one spark plug and forty-two sweatshirts."

PROTEST MARCH

Earl Weaver recorded 1,480 victories in his 17 seasons as skipper of the Baltimore Orioles. As a manager, Weaver was not afraid to exchange heated words with any home-plate umpire in the league. On one occasion, Weaver got into an argument with umpire Ron Luciano. "I'm playing this game under protest," Weaver screamed.

"Protest? On what grounds?" the ump asked.

"On the grounds of your integrity," the Baltimore skipper shouted.

"You know I have to announce the protest," Umpire Luciano replied. "Are you sure that's how you want me to do it?"

"Damn right!" Weaver grumbled. And so the Baltimore Orioles played a Major League baseball game under protest because their manager doubted the home-plate umpire's integrity.

NOW, HEAR THIS

The sounds of silence were sweet to New York Mets outfielder Bobby Bonilla in 1992. To help improve his concentration at the plate, Bonilla took the suggestion of his batting coach and wore earplugs while hitting. The plugs silenced any disturbing sounds that may have distracted Bonilla while he batted, including the boos of the hometown fans who were dissatisfied with Bobby's on-field production as a player that season.

SAY, WHAT?

Frankie Frisch, the manager of the St. Louis Cardinals' famous Gas House Gang, knew how to have fun on the field. One day during a close contest, Frisch began to bug the home-plate umpire. Frankie complained to, yelled at, and badgered the ump inning after inning. However, the Cardinal skipper had enough sense not to do or say anything serious enough to get himself thrown out of the game. Finally, late in the game Frisch shouted something to the ump from the St. Louis dugout. The umpire couldn't make out Frankie's remark. "What did you say, Frisch?" he yelled to the leader of the Gas House Gang.

"Hey," called Frankie Frisch, "you guessed at everything else today. See if you can guess what I just said." Frisch and his players roared in laughter.

"Okay, I will," shouted back the ump. "And for saying it you're out of the game, Frisch!" On the way to the locker room, Frankie Frisch didn't find anything humorous about the umpire's funny reply.

BUTT OUT

Umpire Frank Umont also had some hot exchanges with Earl Weaver. In 1969, Umont ejected the Baltimore skipper for smoking a cigar in the dugout before a game. The next day, Earl Weaver brought the team's lineup card to Frank Umont at home plate—with a candy cigarette dangling from his lips!

MILLER TIME

Having a star player like Babe Ruth on your team can be a mixed blessing, as New York Yankees manager Miller Huggins quickly learned. Ruth, who never paid much attention to training rules or team regulations, made no attempt to hide his off-the-field behavior. Late one night while the Yankees were on the road, Huggins and road secretary Mark Roth were sitting in a hotel lobby when Babe Ruth walked in way after curfew. "I'll have to talk to Ruth tomorrow about the late hours he keeps," Huggins said to Roth.

The next afternoon, the Yankees played a game. In the contest, Babe Ruth clubbed two home runs. That evening Miller Huggins and Mark Roth were again in the hotel lobby when Babe Ruth came strolling in long after curfew.

"He's done it again," Roth said to Huggins. "Are you going to talk to him?"

"I sure am," answered Huggins. As Babe walked by, Miller Huggins yelled out, "Hi, Babe. How are you?"

POOR GUYS

Texas Rangers outfielder Pete Incaviglia tried to make people believe Major League baseball players were not overpaid when he made this funny remark in 1990: "People think we make three or four million dollars a year," said Incaviglia. "They don't realize most of us make only $500,000!"

STOP IT

Baseball funny man Bob Uecker owns up to the fact that he wasn't much of a hitter during his playing days. Uecker claims manager Gene Mauch once said to him, "Get a bat and stop this rally!"

BACKDOOR PLAY

When Dave Winfield was playing outfield for the San Diego Padres, he sometimes had trouble throwing the ball in. Winfield had a cannon for an arm, but often overthrew the cutoff man. To improve his throwing, Dave took extra practice. A short time later, Winfield got a chance to show off his new throwing ability. A ball was lined to right field which Winfield fielded on one hop. Dave needed to make a throw to the plate. Cutoff man Darrel Thomas knew he wouldn't be involved in the throw so he turned his back to Dave to watch what he hoped would be a close play at home. Winfield fired the ball in and hit Darrel Thomas right in the rear end. After the game when Winfield was asked about his wild throw, Dave joked, "Well, at least I finally hit the cutoff man!"

YOU BURN ME UP

Jamie Quirk, of the Kansas City Royals, pulled the ultimate bathroom joke on pitcher Dan Quisenberry while they were in the bullpen in Boston. When Quisenberry went into a portable toilet in the bullpen, Quirk thought it would be funny to light a fire under Dan. He lit some newspapers and smoked Quisenberry out of the portable bathroom. The crowd roared when Dan Quisenberry rushed out and was caught with his pants down!

FAINT HEART

When Nick Altrock was coaching third for the old Washington Senators, he never missed a chance to take a verbal potshot at an umpire. Once during a game a Senators batter hit a line shot foul into the stands behind Altrock. An umpire ran over and saw some people in the stands helping a female spectator who was unconscious. "What happened?" the ump asked Nick. "Did that ball hit her?"

"Nah," answered Nick Altrock. "When you yelled foul, she was so shocked that you finally made a correct call she passed out!"

BOOK NOTES

Hurler Bo Belinsky of the California Angels was famous for dating beautiful women when he wasn't playing baseball. He also had a sense of humor. When he wrote a book about his exploits, he entitled it *Pitching and Wooing.*

FUNNY MONEY

In 1970, Bernie Carbo played for the Cincinnati Reds, who were managed by Sparky Anderson. As a skipper, Sparky strictly enforced team rules and regulations. Whenever a player did something wrong, Anderson was quick to levy a fine. It was also Sparky's habit to donate to charity the money he collected from players in fines. One day, a smiling Bernie Carbo came to the Reds' skipper with a question. "My wife keeps asking me why we get so many thank-you notes from the Heart Fund. She can't figure out why I'm making so many contributions. What should I tell her?" Anderson just laughed and walked away.

KINER QUIPS

New York Mets broadcaster Ralph Kiner, who was a great slugger during his playing days, says some of the funniest things. On one occasion, he remarked, "The Mets' Todd Hundley walked intensely his last time up." On another occasion, the ever glib Kiner cracked, "That's the great thing about baseball. You never know exactly what's going on."

CLOUDING THE ISSUE

Outfield slugger Jackie Jensen of the Boston Red Sox launched baseballs into the clouds in the 1950s, but liked to keep his feet on the ground. Jensen was so afraid of airplane travel that he refused to fly to his team's away games. In fact, Jackie was so afraid of flying that he retired from baseball. He returned to the big leagues only after a year of therapeutic hypnosis, which cured his problem.

A BREATH OF FRESH AIR

Los Angeles Dodgers team captain Maury Wills was great at stealing bases, but terrible at leading team exercises. While pacing his teammates through calisthenics, he once shouted, "Okay everyone, now inhale . . . and then dehale!"

SHAME ON YOU!

Shortstop Johnny Logan, of the old Milwaukee Braves, was asked to pick his number-one Major League ballplayer of all time. Logan, who had a habit of mangling the English language, replied, "Well, I guess I'd have to go with the immoral Babe Ruth."

HEART PROBLEM

When the old Boston Braves manager George Stallings suffered a mild heart attack at the end of the season, his physician asked him about the ailment. "What do you think is the origin of your problem?" the doctor asked Stallings.

George Stallings looked the physician in the eye and replied, "Bases on balls! Bases on balls!"

DON'T BUG ME

Baseball broadcaster Richie Ashburn was a big hitter as a Major League player. His funny remarks are still a big hit with baseball fans. When Richie's playing career was winding down, he played outfield for the young New York Mets. In a game against the Houston Astros, Ashburn encountered swarms of hungry mosquitoes in the Houston outfield. After the game, Richie Ashburn said to reporters, "Houston is the only city in the country where women wear insect repellent instead of perfume."

MOUTHING OFF

After his playing days ended, Frenchy Bordagary tried his hand at being a manager. The daffy ex-Brooklyn Dodger took over as the skipper of a minor league team and before long got into a heated argument with an umpire. Frenchy got so mad that he spit at the ump. For his unsportsmanlike display of anger, Frenchy Bordagary received a 60-day suspension from the league president. When Frenchy was questioned about his suspension he had this to say: "Okay, maybe I did wrong," Frenchy admitted, "but the punishment is more than I expectorated."

SEE YA

Major League baseball umpires have been the target of many wisecracks over the years. Players argue with them. Managers and coaches complain about their calls. Even the fans criticize the men in blue. Way back in 1942, Gladys Gooding, the stadium organist at Ebbets Field, the home of the Brooklyn Dodgers, got into the act. As the umpires walked out on the field one day, Gladys played "Three Blind Mice."

THINGS ARE LOOKING UP

Outfielder and sometimes first baseman Carmelo Martinez took a humorous approach to analyzing his ability as a defensive player. He once told a reporter, "In the outfield, fly balls are my only weakness."

TRY TO UNDERSTAND

Many years ago when the Chicago Cubs won the National League pennant, a player named Woody English was captain of the team. A Chicago newspaper wanted to capitalize on the event, so it paid Woody to write a daily story about the World Series the Cubs were in. Of course, English didn't really write the story. He just scribbled some notes, which were then written up into story material by a professional ghostwriter the newspaper hired. After a few stories appeared in the paper, the ghostwriter showed up in the Cubs' locker room one day to visit with English. When Woody saw the writer approaching, he yelled, "Hey, buddy, quit using all those big words. I can't understand what I'm writing."

MEDICAL MIRTH

Milwaukee Brewers broadcaster Bob Uecker was scheduled to have life-threatening surgery for two aneurysms in his abdominal aorta in 1991. Despite the seriousness of the medical procedure, Uecker broadcast a baseball game just three days before the surgery. When asked why he did it, Bob Uecker joked, "I have an aneurysm clause in my contract. If you work with an aneurysm you get a bonus." The funny story had a happy ending as Bob Uecker recovered completely.

DOCK HIS PAY

When Andy Van Slyke was a member of the Pittsburgh Pirates, his team was somewhat weak defensively. Van Slyke once described his team's ability in the field by joking, "They had better defense at Pearl Harbor."

THE PUPPET MASTER

In 1995, outfielder Andy Van Slyke, then a member of the Philadelphia Phillies, had a slight disagreement with a team mascot. In the heat of the moment, Van Slyke hit the mascot Bert from the children's television show "Sesame Street." Van Slyke thought the incident was forgotten until he stepped to the plate for a game in Pittsburgh a few days later. As soon as he appeared, the stadium organist began to play the popular "Sesame Street" theme as a gag.

KINGS OF DIAMOND DAFFINESS

CHARLES "CASEY" STENGEL

Charles Stengel was a daffy outfielder in his playing days, which were spent with the Brooklyn Dodgers, the Philadelphia Phillies, the New York Giants, and other clubs. He also managed the Boston Braves, the Brooklyn Dodgers, the New York Yankees, and the New York Mets. It was Casey's skill as a manager that got him into the Baseball Hall of Fame. He won the World Championship several times at the helm of the New York Yankees. However, Casey is best remembered for his baffling choice of wacky words and his weird way of explaining things that became known as "Stengelese."

Different, But the Same

Casey Stengel was asked to compare second baseman Billy Martin of the New York Yankees to second baseman Nellie Fox of the Chicago White Sox. In his best Stengelese, Casey replied, "They're very much alike in a lot of similarities."

Age Wise

Casey Stengel had this to say when he first saw future Hall-of-Famer catcher Johnny Bench: "He's the best 23-year-old catcher I've seen since Campy [meaning Roy Campanella], and Campy was 25 years old the first time I saw him."

The Gag That Bombed

In 1916, young Casey Stengel was a member of the wacky Brooklyn Dodgers squad managed by future Hall-of-Famer Wilbert Robinson. Robinson, an outstanding catcher with the old Baltimore Orioles, had carved his niche in the baseball record book on June 10, 1892, when he collected seven hits (six singles and a double) in seven times at bat.

Wilbert constantly reminded his collection of diamond clowns of his many personal achievements as a player, especially his exceptional ability to catch towering pop-ups while behind the plate. Wilbert Robinson wasn't really a braggart; he just wanted to impress upon his young players that he knew what he was talking about when he gave them advice as a manager.

However, jokester Casey Stengel used Robinson's own words as bait for one of baseball's great practical jokes. Stengel, with the aid of his teammates, goaded their manager into making a really wacky wager. He bet Wilbert he couldn't catch a baseball dropped from an airplane circling above the field. With his reputation as a "guy who could catch anything" on the line, Wilbert Robinson agreed to the bet. He was determined to prove to Casey and his cohorts what a great catcher he was.

The day of the aerial baseball bombing finally came. Ruth Law, one of America's famous female aviators, was hired to pilot a plane with an open cockpit. In the aircraft with her was Casey Stengel. Standing far below on the Dodgers' training field in Florida was Wilbert Robinson, wearing his catcher's mitt. Looking on were members of the Dodgers team. When Wilbert was ready to attempt his crazy catch, he signaled the plane above.

It was then that sneaky Stengel pulled a shifty switcheroo. Instead of a baseball, he dropped a grapefruit out of the plane. From far below the grapefruit looked just like a ball.

As the grapefruit plummeted toward the baseball field, Wilbert Robinson positioned himself directly in its path. The grapefruit slipped through Robertson's outstretched arms, hit him squarely in the chest, and exploded! The force of the impact knocked the Dodgers manager to the ground, where he lay dazed for several seconds. When Wilbert Robinson regained his senses, his chest was soaked with juice and splattered

with squishy sections of grapefruit. Thinking the worst, the future Hall-of-Famer panicked.

"Help me!" he screamed to the surrounding Dodger players, who were already laughing hysterically. "Help me! I'm dying! The ball split my chest open and I'm bleeding to death!"

When the players continued to howl, Wilbert Robinson smelled a rat, a rat by the name of Stengel. He sat up and, upon quick examination, learned that the only injuries he'd suffered were a bruised ego and a fractured grapefruit. Thanks to kooky Casey Stengel's wacky prank, everyone on the Dodgers squad had a good laugh at their manager's expense. However, Robinson was so infuriated, young Casey had to stay in hiding for several days until the manager forgave Stengel for pulling off one of baseball's funniest gags.

Give Him a Hand

Bobby Brown, who later became the American League president, was a target of one of Casey's barbs. Brown had played in the majors as a third baseman and established a reputation as a great hitter and a lousy fielder. Said Casey of Bobby Brown's ability: "He reminds me of a fella who's been hitting for twelve years and fielding for one."

Who's Tired?

Manager Casey Stengel was armed with a quick wit and was always ready to fire off a fast one-liner. On one occasion, the Yankee manager waddled out to the mound to yank a weary pitcher out of the game. "But, Skip," protested the pitcher, who was reluctant to leave, "I'm not tired."

Casey eyed the young hurler and took the baseball from him. "Well, I'm tired of you," Stengel replied as he signaled the bullpen for a relief pitcher.

Mental Problem

Duke Snider, the great Dodger centerfielder, loved to listen to Casey spout Stengelese. However, at one point it did cause him some concern. "I got to where I could understand Casey real well," said Snider. "That sort of worried me."

Three Tries

When Casey was the manager of the New York Mets, one of his players was Marvelous Marv Throneberry, a fan favorite who never became a great Major League player. However, the hapless Marv was almost as zany as Ol' Casey.

During the 1962 season, Throneberry came to the plate late in a game against the Chicago Cubs. There were two outs and the bases were loaded. When Marvelous Marv hit what appeared to be a game-winning triple, no one was more surprised or happier than Casey Stengel. Casey jumped up and down, and clapped and cheered. He was so busy celebrating that he never noticed that Marvelous Marv missed first base in his haste to get to third. However, almost everyone else in the ballpark noticed Marv's mistake, including the Cubs.

When the Cubs' pitcher tossed the ball to first base, Throneberry was called out. Stengel shot out of the dugout in a rage. He stalked up to the umpire and began to dispute the call.

"Calm down, Casey," said the ump. "Not only did he miss first, he missed second, too."

Casey, who was never at a loss for words, quickly fired back, "Well, I know damn well he didn't miss third. He's standing on it!"

Bird Brainer

Casey Stengel played some of his best baseball during his years with the old Brooklyn Dodgers. When Stengel was traded to Brooklyn's National League rival, the Pittsburgh Pirates, he knew he'd get booed the first time the Pirates visited the Dodgers. Of course, Casey wasn't the type to take getting booed lying down. When Pittsburgh arrived at Brooklyn's Ebbets Field, Casey cooked up a classic gag guaranteed to please even the rowdy Dodger rooters. When the stadium announcer introduced Casey as a starting outfielder for the Pirates,

Stengel hopped out of the dugout. As the Dodger fans began to boo loudly, Casey bowed and tipped his hat. As he raised the cap from his head, a sparrow flew off of his brow and winged its way skyward. The wacky bird-brained stunt quickly won over the hostile crowd. The fans clapped and cheered the return of one of the game's zaniest players . . . nutty Casey Stengel.

Fired Up

Casey Stengel wasn't the type of guy to take complaints lying down. When the New York Yankees traded hurler Mickey McDermott, McDermott complained that manager Stengel never gave him enough chances to pitch. When Stengel heard about Mickey's remark, he was quick to reply in kind. "I noticed whenever anyone gave Mickey McDermott enough chances to pitch," said Casey, "a lot of managers got fired."

Private Eye

When young Casey Stengel was a member of the New York Giants, he quickly earned a reputation as a troublemaker. Stengel, along with his teammate Irish Meusel, spent many late nights roaming the town. Things got so bad that the New York Giants' manager, John McGraw, finally hired a special detective to follow Stengel and Meusel around at night to keep them out of trouble. When Stengel learned about the detective, he angrily went to McGraw. "What's the big idea of hiring a detective to follow me and Meusel?" Casey roared. "I don't deserve to be treated like that."

"Oh," said McGraw, "and how should you be treated?"

"I should have my own private detective just to follow me," Casey replied.

Smart Mouth

Pitcher Warren Spahn played for the Boston Braves in 1940 when Casey Stengel was the team manager, and also for the New York Mets in the 1960s when Casey managed that team. Spahn, himself a quick wit, once said, "I'm probably the only guy who played for Stengel before and after he was a genius."

Wild Pitch

The "old perfessor" once said this about fastball pitcher Rex Barney of the Dodgers, who had difficulty throwing strikes: "He has the power to throw the ball through a wall," said Casey, "but you couldn't be quite sure which building."

Injury Problem

One year when Casey Stengel was the manager of the World Champion New York Yankees, his team was plagued by a rash of injuries. Every day someone new got hurt. Finally, one afternoon Stengel was on the bench when he heard shortstop Phil Rizzuto chatting with third baseman Bobby Brown. "When the baby cried this morning, my wife jumped out of bed and fell flat on the floor," Rizzuto said. "I thought it was funny until I learned she broke two of her toes."

Casey threw his arms up in disgust. "Did you hear that?" he yelled to the rest of the Yankee team. "Boy, this is a rough season! Even the wives are getting hurt!"

Instant Replay

When Casey Stengel was the manager of the Brooklyn Dodgers, he had a pitcher named Walter "Boom Boom" Beck and an outfielder named Hack Wilson on his squad. Beck wasn't that great a hurler, but Wilson was one of the game's greatest hitters.

When the Dodgers met the Philadelphia Phillies one afternoon, Beck was on the mound and Wilson was in right field. The batters immediately started to blast pitch after pitch from Beck. The balls careened off the outfield fence near Wilson. Time after time, Hack scooped up the ball and fired it back into second base.

Casey soon tired of Boom Boom and went out to yank the Brooklyn hurler. While Stengel and Beck conferred on the mound, right fielder Hack Wilson relaxed in his position. He rested with his hands on his knees, his head down, and his eyes staring at the ground. Somehow Boom Boom Beck convinced Casey to leave him in the game. As soon as Beck started to pitch again, baseballs flew toward the outfield wall.

Boom! The balls bounced off the wall. Hack Wilson fielded them on a bounce and fired them into second. Soon Casey Stengel made another trek to the mound. Wilson relaxed in the outfield with his head down as Casey and Beck talked things over. Amazingly, Boom Boom again talked Stengel into giving him one last shot against the Philly batters. Boom! Boom! Hack Wilson played the bounce and fired the balls into second base.

Finally, Casey Stengel had seen enough. He called "time-out" and dashed out to the mound. "Give me the ball, Walt," he demanded. Beck refused. Meanwhile, out in the outfield Hack Wilson was resting with his hands on his knees and his head down. He didn't even glance toward the infield where Stengel and Beck were arguing. "Give me the ball!" Casey yelled.

"You want it," answered Beck. "Here!" He reached back and fired the ball into right field. Boom! It smacked against the wall. Hearing that familiar sound sent Hack Wilson into action. He ran after the ball, scooped it up, and fired it into second, never realizing play had not yet resumed.

What a Kick!

One day Walter Boom-Boom Beck was having his usual run of bad luck on the mound. Opposing batters blasted pitch after pitch. When the side was finally retired, Beck stormed into the Brooklyn Dodgers' dugout. In a fit of anger, Boom Boom kicked the water cooler. "Hey, calm down! Don't do that," called manager Casey Stengel. Beck smiled, expecting to hear some words of encouragement from Casey. "If you break your leg," Stengel continued, "I won't be able to trade you."

Fan Chatter

One day in the middle of a game, Casey Stengel walked out of the New York dugout and headed for the pitcher's mound. He planned to remove a Yankee hurler who was getting belted by hitter after hitter. When he reached the mound, the pitcher begged Casey to keep him in the game. "Why do I have to leave the game?" the hurler asked.

Casey snatched the ball out of the pitcher's hand and pointed to the fans in the stands. "Because," explained Casey, "up there people are beginning to talk."

LEO "THE LIP" DUROCHER

Leo Durocher loved to argue with umpires, and he loved fine clothes. Durocher, who excelled as both a Major League player and manager, once said, "Anyone who doesn't change his shirt three times a day is a slob."

Vegetable Scoop

Once when he was served a big salad, Leo Durocher refused to taste it. "I never eat the stuff," he explained. "It makes your bones soft."

Mr. Nice Guy?

Sports announcer Red Barber once interviewed Leo Durocher when the Lip was managing the Brooklyn Dodgers. The day before the interview, the Dodgers had lost to the New York Giants because several Giants players had crashed home runs. Durocher referred to the homers as cheap shots, and Barber asked him about his comments. "Why don't you admit they were legitimate home runs?" Red Barber asked Leo. "Why don't you be a nice guy for a change?"

The irascible Leo the Lip scowled at Barber and then

shouted, "A nice guy? I'm not a nice guy and I'm in first place! Take it from me, nice guys finish last!"

Fall Guy

How fierce a competitor was Leo Durocher? He once said he'd trip his grandmother rounding third base if it meant a victory!

Dressed to Win

It was a well-known fact that Leo the Lip liked to be well dressed. Durocher was also extremely superstitious. When he was managing, he kept notes about what combinations of clothes he wore to the ballpark. If his team lost a game, the clothing combination he wore that day was never repeated.

Knocked Out

Leo Durocher was famous for staging lengthy disputes with umpires. However, umpire George Magerkurth once got the best of Lippy Leo. During the course of an important game, manager Durocher was constantly complaining about Magerkurth's calls. Finally, the ump had enough. "One more word out of you, Durocher, and you're out of the game," umpire Magerkurth threatened. Since Leo didn't want to get thrown out, he shut up.

A short time later, one of Durocher's players was called out by Magerkurth on a close play at first. Leo raced out of the dugout. Without saying a word, he grabbed his chest and pretended to faint on the playing field right in front of umpire George Magerkurth. Magerkurth bent over the motionless form of Leo the Lip and shouted, "The runner is still out. And you, Durocher, whether you're dead or alive, you're out of the game, too!"

Cool Response

Willie Mays was a member of the New York Giants team managed by Leo Durocher in the 1950s. One afternoon in Pittsburgh, centerfielder Mays made an astounding catch against the Pirates' Rocky Nelson. Nelson crushed a Sal Maglie fastball and sent it sailing straight over the head of Willie Mays in the outfield. Mays raced back, jumped up, and snared the ball with his bare hand for the third out of the inning.

In the Giants' dugout, the players were going wild over the spectacular grab made by Willie. "Don't anyone say anything to Mays," Durocher said as Willie trotted in. When Willie Mays entered the dugout, he found Durocher by the water cooler and the rest of the team deathly silent.

"Damn! Isn't anyone going to say anything?" Willie asked.

"Why?" replied Leo. "What happened?"

"I just made a pretty good catch," Willie explained.

"Gee wiz, I was at the watercooler," answered Leo the Lip. "I guess I missed it. You'll just have to make another one next inning."

BILL VEECK

Bill Veeck was the P.T. Barnum of Major League baseball. As the owner of the old St. Louis Browns and the president of the Chicago White Sox, Veeck pulled off some of the wildest and funniest stunts in baseball history.

Cool Idea

Bill Veeck had a shower installed in Chicago's centerfield bleachers in 1977 so fans could cool off on hot days.

Every Guy's Game

When Bill Veeck became president of the Chicago White Sox in 1976 after a short absence from the baseball scene, he quickly sounded the praises of his favorite game. "Baseball is the only game left for people," said Veeck. "To play basketball now you have to be 7 feet tall. To play football, you have to be the same width!"

Ka-Boom!

The first exploding scoreboard was the brainchild of Bill Veeck. The scoreboard was installed in Chicago, and fireworks exploded every time a White Sox player belted a home run!

Veeck's Files and UFOs

In 1959, the UFO craze was sweeping the country. People everywhere were concerned about alien spacecraft and invaders from Mars. In Chicago, Bill Veeck was running the Chicago White Sox and used the lure of space aliens to stage a wild publicity stunt. On the 1959 roster of the White Sox were Nellie Fox and Luis Aparicio, two of the smallest players in the Major Leagues at the time. Bill Veeck arranged for "Martians" to land at the ballpark to kidnap Fox and Aparicio before the start of a game.

Here's what happened the day Bill Veeck's Martians invaded Chicago: After Nellie Fox and Luis Aparicio were introduced by the stadium announcer, the two White Sox players took the field. Out of the clouds above the stadium a strange helicopter appeared. As the crowd in the stands cheered, the helicopter landed in the infield. Out of the craft jumped three tiny men dressed in spacesuits and wearing space helmets. They were introduced as little men from Mars.

As the crowd roared in delight, the Martians captured Nellie Fox and Luis Aparicio. The men from Mars dragged their captive earthmen over to a microphone. The crowd applauded wildly as Fox and Aparicio were made "honorary Martians," sworn to help their adopted alien brothers in their never-ending struggle against other "Earth Giants."

The crowd loved every minute of the wild publicity stunt Bill Veeck had arranged. The Chicago players must have appreciated it too, because the White Sox went on to win the American League pennant that year.

Short Game Stopper

The 1951 St. Louis Browns team owned by Bill Veeck and managed by Zack Taylor had some problems. The Browns were in last place in the league and had trouble drawing fans to their games. Showman Bill Veeck decided to spice up the Browns' contests by staging some publicity stunts. One of his all-time best stunts was signing Eddie Gaedel to play for the Browns as a pinch hitter.

Gaedel became famous in the second game of a doubleheader played between the Browns and the Detroit Tigers at St. Louis in 1951. Eddie Gaedel didn't become a baseball hero for swinging a big bat. He became famous as the smallest man to ever bat in the Major

Leagues. Gaedel stood only three feet, seven inches tall and wore the fraction 1/8 on his back as his number. Since Veeck had listed Gaedel on the official St. Louis roster, the umpire had to let Eddie bat even though the Tigers protested.

Little Eddie Gaedel walked on four straight balls. As the crowd laughed hysterically and cheered loudly, Gaedel trotted down to first base. He was quickly replaced in the game by pinch runner Jim Delsing. The crowd gave Eddie Gaedel a loud ovation as he left the field, never to return. Gaedel never batted in another Major League game, but Bill Veeck's little trick on the Tigers was a big success.

VERNON "LEFTY, GOOFY" GOMEZ

Hall-of-Fame hurler Lefty Goofy Gomez played for the New York Yankees in the 1930s and 1940s. In his thirteen seasons as a Yankee, he had only one losing season. As a funny man on the mound, he was never at a loss for producing laughs.

The Naked Truth

One day when the New York Yankees traveled to Boston to play the Red Sox, Lefty Gomez was scheduled to be the starting pitcher in the small, confined Fenway Park. However, when Yankee manager Joe McCarthy went looking for his starter, he couldn't find Gomez in the locker room. After a hasty search of the surrounding area, Joe finally found Lefty. Gomez was crouched in a phone booth, and he was totally naked. "I'm staying in here until game time," explained Lefty. "That way, when I get out on the field Fenway will look real big to me."

Catch Phrase

Once Lefty Gomez was scheduled to pitch an exhibition game for a team with money problems. In fact, the first baseman on Gomez's squad was in serious trouble with the Internal Revenue Service. It was rumored that the first baseman might even be arrested. "How do you feel about pitching when your first baseman might be in jail when the game starts?" a reporter asked Lefty Gomez.

After a moment of silence, Lefty replied, "Well, it'll be an awful long throw for our shortstop."

Bright Guy

One dark and dismal afternoon, the New York Yankees took on the Cleveland Indians in a game that pitted Yankee pitcher Lefty Gomez against the Indians' ace fastballer, Bob Feller. Feller was one of the hardest throwers to ever hurl a baseball in the Major Leagues. On occasion, some of Feller's pitches went just a bit wild. No batter in his right mind wanted to get "beaned" by one of Bob's blazing bullets. As the skies darkened that gloomy afternoon and the visibility became worse and worse, some of the Yankee hitters started to worry about such a beaning.

Late in the game, Lefty Gomez stepped up to the

ARE YOU SURE HE CAN SEE ME?

plate. The field was now covered in shadows. As Bob Feller started to wind up, Lefty lowered his bat, took out a match, and lit it. Gomez held up the burning match to the astonishment of the home-plate umpire. "What are you doing Gomez?" barked the ump. "Can't you see Feller is getting ready to pitch?"

"I can see Feller fine," Lefty replied. "I just want to make sure he can see me!"

Fish Story

While traveling on a train with his Yankee teammates, Lefty Gomez was informed by reporters that Albert Einstein was also aboard the same train. Gomez considered Einstein an inventor, and bragged about an invention of his own. "I invented a fish bowl that adds ten years to the lives of tropical fish," Gomez told the group of interested reporters. "The bowl rotates. That way, the fish don't have to waste energy swimming around. They just sit there and the bowl does all the work."

Batty

Lefty Gomez was always a weak hitter at best. Nevertheless, he never passed over a chance to talk about his prowess at the plate. He once said, "I tried to knock dirt out of my spikes with a bat the way the big hitters do, and I cracked myself in the ankle and broke a bone!"

Apply Yourself

When Lefty Gomez retired from baseball, he filled out an application for a new job. One of the questions on the application was, Why did you leave your last position? Jokester Lefty Gomez wrote in response, "I couldn't get the side out!"

A Sign of the Times

Pitcher Lefty Gomez and catcher Bill Dickey were battery mates for the New York Yankees in a game against the Boston Red Sox. At the plate for the Sox was home-run slugger Jimmy Foxx, a very dangerous hitter. Dickey gave Gomez the fastball sign. Gomez shook off the sign and refused to throw Foxx a fastball. Next, catcher Bill Dickey flashed the sign for a curve ball. Again, Lefty Gomez shook off the sign. Next, Dickey signaled for a change-up. Gomez shook his head and refused to throw a change-up. Bill Dickey called "time-out" and stormed

out to the mound. "Well, just what do you want to throw him!" Dickey yelled angrily to Gomez.

Lefty smiled and said, "To tell you the truth, I'd just as soon not throw him anything."

Pay Day

Lefty Gomez had lots of funny stories about the days he spent pitching in the minor leagues. One of his zany tales was about money problems. Lefty was staying in a boarding house and, due to lack of funds, got way behind in his rent. When the landlady demanded payment, Goofy Gomez tried to talk his way out of the jam. "Just think," Lefty said to the landlady. "Someday you'll be able to say Lefty Gomez the great pitcher once lived here."

The landlady wasn't impressed. According to Lefty's account she answered, "I know . . . and if you don't pay me I'll be able to say it tomorrow."

Full, Thanks

After Lefty Gomez pitched himself into trouble by loading the bases, New York manager Joe McCarthy called time and walked out to the mound. "I just want you to know the bases are full," said Joe.

"Did you think I thought those guys were extra infielders?" Gomez replied.

Throwing the Bull

Late in his career, Lefty Gomez was traded to the Boston Braves, who were managed by Casey Stengel. "The trouble with you," Casey told Lefty, "is you're not throwing as hard as you used to."

"You're wrong," Gomez answered. "I'm throwing twice as hard, but the ball is only going half as fast."

BASEBALL'S FUNNY BUSINESS

KISS OFF

New York pitcher Scott Kamieniecki found himself struggling on the mound in the second inning of a game against the California Angels in 1991. The Yanks were leading 2–1, but the Angels had two men on base. Kamieniecki expected a visit on the mound from the New York pitching coach. What he got instead was a visit from an exotic, well-endowed dancer named Toppsy Curvey, who jumped out of the stands and raced up to the Yankee pitcher. Ms. Curvey threw her arms around Scott Kamieniecki and gave him a big hug and kiss before she was escorted off the field by stadium security guards. Before she exited the diamond, dancer Toppsy Curvey wished pitcher Scott Kamieniecki "good luck." But Kamieniecki didn't enjoy any luck that day. The Angels ended up winning the game and Scott Kamieniecki was the losing pitcher.

SPACED OUT

Bill Lee, who pitched for the Boston Red Sox and the Montreal Expos, was nicknamed "Spaceman" because of his out-of-this world remarks and attitudes. He once angered the entire California Angels team by summing up their combined ability at the plate this way: "The California Angels," said Lee, "couldn't break a chandelier if they held batting practice in a hotel lobby."

HANDS OFF

In 1980, Minnesota Twins manager Gene Mauch was asked why he left starting pitcher Pete Redfern in a game for four innings when Redfern struggled on the mound in every inning. Said Mauch as he smirked, "I was afraid I might choke him if I had him in the dugout!"

PASSED OUT

On his way to the ballpark one afternoon, John Mc-Graw, the manager of the New York Giants, was stopped by a fan. McGraw, who had a reputation for being gruff, didn't waste time exchanging pleasantries with the fan. "What do you want?" McGraw barked.

"How about a pass for today's game?" asked the fan politely.

"Why should I give you a pass?" the Giants skipper demanded.

"Well, I'm a friend of the umpire Bill Klem," the friend replied.

"A friend of umpire Bill Klem!" roared John Mc-Graw. "No pass for you, you liar!"

The astonished fan gasped. "Liar?" he sputtered. "What do you mean?"

"Humph!" grunted McGraw. "I never knew an umpire who had a friend."

MAD MAN

Al Hrabosky, who pitched for the Atlanta Braves in the 1980s, was often called the "Mad Hungarian"! Hrabosky earned his nickname by talking to himself during games and by stomping around the pitching mound like a man possessed.

MARRIED TO BASEBALL

Don Zimmer spent most of his life actively involved in Major League baseball as a player, coach, and manager. In fact, he married his wife Jean (nicknamed "Soot") at home plate in a baseball stadium in Elmira, New York. The wedding took place at a night game on August 16, 1951.

COLOR BLIND

Catcher Yogi Berra once described the numerous sweaters he owned. "The only color I don't have," explained Yogi, "is navy brown."

HOUSE SITTER

In 1978, the Boston Red Sox, managed by Don Zimmer, met the New York Yankees in a one-game playoff to determine the American League's East Division champion. The game was won by the Yankees on a home run hit by New York shortstop Bucky Dent. In 1983, Don Zimmer was hired as a coach by the New York Yankees, and Bucky Dent was traded from the Yankees to the Texas Rangers. Since Zimmer needed a place to live near New York, he rented Bucky Dent's vacant house in New Jersey. When the Zimmers moved into the Dent's home, they found photographs of Bucky's game-winning home-run hit against the Red Sox in 1978 hanging on walls all around the house. The first thing Don Zimmer did was turn around the photographs of Dent's famous hit, so they all faced the wall!

TIME TO GO

The 1989 National League Manager of the Year was Don Zimmer of the Chicago Cubs. Zimmer spent forty-seven years in baseball, thirty-five of them in the Major Leagues (12 as a player, 13 as a manager, and 10 as a coach). In 1995, Don was a coach with the Colorado Rockies, when he decided enough was enough. Zimmer retired from baseball June 6, 1995, and did it in the middle of a ball game. Don Zimmer quit Major League baseball in the fifth inning of Colorado's 5–4 victory over the St. Louis Cardinals. "Zim" just walked off the field and never looked back.

DROP IT!

Tommy Lasorda, the manager of the Los Angeles Dodgers, has some strange ideas about good luck. Lasorda believed seeing pigeon droppings or a pregnant lady before a game was good luck.

AUDIO TAPE

Outfielders Willie Wilson and Daniel Garcia of the Kansas City Royals taped their mouths shut and stood stiffly at attention while the National Anthem was played before their game against the Seattle Mariners on May 26, 1981. Wilson and Garcia pulled the stunt hoping it would help end the Royals' season-long slump.

CRAZY QUESTION

The Detroit Tigers met the St. Louis Cardinals in the 1934 World Series. The Cardinals club, coached by Frankie Frisch, was a mixed bag of baseball nuts which included Dizzy Dean, his brother Daffy, and Leo "The Lip" Durocher. Before the first game of the series, Frisch held a team meeting to tell his players where they should be positioned defensively for each of the Detroit hitters. When he finished, Frisch asked, "Any questions?"

Durocher shook his head. Dizzy and Daffy remained silent. Suddenly infielder Pepper Martin raised his hand and stood up. "I have a question, Skipper," said Martin very seriously. "Should I paint my new racing car red with black wheels or black with red wheels?"

IT'S YOUR CALL

Major League umpire Ron Luciano was asked to rate the five most difficult Major League managers he ever had to deal with. After very little thought, Luciano rated manager Earl Weaver of the Baltimore Orioles numbers one to four. His fifth choice was skipper Frank Robinson. When questioned about his choice of Robinson, Ron Luciano explained, "He's Earl's protégé!"

IN REVERSE

Zany! That is the only way to describe Jimmy Piersall. In his Major League playing days, Piersall pulled some really wacky stunts. Perhaps the best of his many gags was the way he celebrated hitting the 100th home run of his Major League career. It happened at the old Polo Grounds in 1963 when Jimmy was a member of the New York Mets. Piersall celebrated his four-sacker feat by running the bases while facing backwards. After Jimmy Piersall's nutty base-running exhibition, Major League baseball's rules committee outlawed backward base running.

DOZE GUYS

Fabulous Faye Throneberry (the brother of Marvelous Marve Throneberry of the New York Mets) was a member of the California Angels in 1979. During one very close, intense game, manager Bill Rigney needed a pinch hitter. Since the fate of the game hung in the balance, Rigney thought over his options and decided on Fabulous Faye. Rigney yelled out Throneberry's name and received no response. When he looked for Fabulous Faye, he found his chosen pinch hitter fast asleep in a corner of the dugout.

BLESS YOU

In 1991 Tim Burke, a pitcher for the New York Mets who was also a Born Again Christian, was asked if religious beliefs could affect a player's attitude on the baseball diamond. Burke replied, "If Jesus were on the field, he'd be pitching inside and breaking up double plays."

A HIT WITH THE JOKES

Al Schacht was known as the Clown Prince of Baseball because of the funny stories he told about the game. "I once ran into an old Major Leaguer on the streets of a big city," Schacht said. "The guy started to brag about his hitting ability as we walked down the street. According to the old-timer, his lifetime average was .390."

"My average would have been .750 if the pitchers weren't afraid to pitch to me," the guy supposedly told Schacht as they stopped at the corner and waited for the light to change. As it changed, the word "Walk" lit up on the sign. "See," said the guy, "they're still afraid of me!"

CLOSE SHAVE

Former Major League relief pitcher Mitch Williams wasn't afraid to be different. Williams said he threw "like a man with his hair on fire." Mitch also sported a tattoo of cartoon character "Speedy Gonzales" on his leg and only trimmed his beard every time he recorded exactly 11 saves.

AWARD-WINNING COMMENT

Johnny Logan, the language-mangling shortstop of the Milwaukee Braves, received an award and was required to make an acceptance speech. "I will perish this trophy forever," stated Logan in a most humble way.

HOT JOKE

Another of Al Schacht's diamond tales deals with a conversation about baseball between Saint Peter and the Devil himself. The talk turned to who could field a better baseball team, and the two got into a heated debate. "Just remember," said St. Peter. "We've got guys like Babe Ruth, Lou Gehrig, and Roger Hornsby playing on our side."

The Devil nodded slyly. "True," he admitted. "But we've got all the umpires on our side."

DAVE THE RAVE

In 1991, All-Star sluggers Dave Parker and Dave Winfield batted side by side in the California Angels batting order. Since both Parker and Winfield are hitters feared by pitchers, someone asked Winfield what he thought about batting in front of Parker. In response, Winfield joked, "You're going to hear pitchers saying, 'Nobody told me there'd be Daves like this'!"

BACK CHECK

Satchel Paige was a great pitcher in both the Negro Leagues and the Major Leagues. Paige often dished out free advice. He once said, "Don't look back! Something might be gaining on you."

DON'T PICK ON ME

Shortstop U.L. Washington of the Kansas City Royals had a funny habit. He didn't chew gum or use chewing tobacco. Washington always played baseball with a toothpick clenched between his teeth!

ROYAL TREATMENT

When Dan Quisenberry was pitching for the Kansas City Royals, he watched in terror as his outfielders made a series of bad plays game after game. Finally, Quisenberry came up with a humorous suggestion for improving the Royals' outfield play. "Our fielders have to catch a lot of balls," said Quisenberry, "or at least deflect them so someone else can."

ROLE PLAYER

Centerfielder Willie Mays never considered himself an actor, but from time to time he appeared on various television shows. On one occasion, Willie was scheduled to appear on a popular television show in a cameo role as himself. When he arrived, the director asked Mays how he planned to play himself. "I don't know," joked Willie. "Just turn those cameras on and if it ain't me, let me know."

WELL-RESTED

In game six of the 1991 World Series, Minnesota Twins player Kirby Puckett had a fantastic game. He tripled, hit a towering sacrifice fly, and homered. To top things off, he made a rally-ending catch by leaping into the wall in centerfield to snare a fly ball. After the game ended in a victory for the Twins, Puckett was asked if he was tired. "I'll get my rest when I'm dead," Kirby joked.

CATCH PHRASE

Dean Chance was on the mound for the California Angels in a close game against the Minnesota Twins. Chance's battery mate was catcher Hank Foiles. The Angels held a slim lead, but the Twins had the bases loaded. Dean Chance fired a sinking fastball low and outside. Catcher Hank Foiles reached out to catch it, and then jumped up and raced back to the screen to chase down what he figured was a wild pitch. As Foiles frantically searched for the ball, all three Twins runners scored. The ball seemed to vanish off the face of the earth. It wasn't until the crazy catcher looked into his glove that he realized the ball had never gotten by him. It was wedged in the pocket of his glove the entire time. Foiles only thought he'd missed it!

CAR SICK HUMOR

Satchel Paige never shied away from compliments or publicity, but a newspaper story about him once got him angry. The story appeared when Paige arrived in the Major Leagues in 1948. The article claimed that Satchel Paige owned a big, red car with the words "Satchel Paige, World's Greatest Pitcher" printed on its side.

"Now, that story isn't true," Satchel complained to his teammates. "I don't own a red car, it's maroon!"

WELL, MOW ME DOWN

When Texas Rangers pitcher Jim Kern was in the minor leagues as a youngster, the older players on the team kept telling him his baseball glove was eating grass. Kern, who refused to be victimized by a prank, just ignored his teammates. However, when he picked up his mitt he found fistfuls of grass stuffed up into the glove's fingerholes.

WORK OF ART

In the 1950s, the St. Louis Cardinals outfield consisted of Del Ennis, Chuck Harmon, and Wally Moon. Ennis, Harmon, and Moon were good players, but they all lacked one vital ability. "The Cardinals have a *Venus de Milo* outfield," a sportswriter once said. "It's beautiful—but no arms."

POOR TASTE

A Major League hitter in the National League once said this about pitcher Fernando Valenzuela: "Valenzuela has three different screwballs," he stated. "The toughest to hit breaks down the middle with an enchilada on it!"

MEAL TICKET

Cletus "Boots" Poffenberger spent most of his professional baseball career in the minor leagues. Nevertheless, Boots was one of the game's craziest characters. Once after he'd been called up from the minors to play for the Detroit Tigers, he checked into a fancy hotel. Poffenberger quickly dialed room service. "Send up the breakfast of champions," Boots said . . . and then clarified his statement by ordering six cold beers and a steak sandwich.

LAUGHTER, THE BEST MEDICINE

You certainly don't have to be a brain surgeon to be a Major League baseball player. Catcher Mickey Sasser proved that when he said he realized his pregnant wife was in labor after he spoke with her physician. "I called the doctor," Sasser explained, "and he told me the contraptions were an hour apart."

SKIP IT, SKIPPER

George "Birdie" Tebbetts, a skipper for the Cincinnati Reds and the Milwaukee Braves, had a philosophical but funny attitude about the role of a Major League manager. "Managing a ball club," Tebbetts said, "is a job for which a man works, studies, hopes, and, if he's so inclined, prays for—knowing all the time that if he gets it he's bound, in the end, to be fired."

KNUCKLEHEAD

A reporter asked Minnesota Twins slugger Harmon Killebrew the best way to hit a knuckleball. "Look for the seams," directed Killebrew, "and then hit in-between them."

A STAR IS BORN

When Wes Ferrell was pitching for the Houston Astros in the Major Leagues, he was a student of the stars. Ferrell believed in astrology and always tried to get his starting assignments on the mound to coincide with his astrological "lucky days."

WRITE THIS DOWN

Pitcher Larry Anderson of the San Diego Padres provided lots of comic relief for his team. He was on the bench one day when he turned to a teammate and asked, "How do you know when your pen runs out of invisible ink?"

FUNNY FOLLOWING

Max Patkin played in the minor leagues as a pitcher, but is best known in baseball circles for his zany clowning on the diamond. He once served as a "clown" coach for Bill Veeck's Cleveland Indians team.

Max's career as a diamond clown began by accident. Patkin was pitching in a service game in Honolulu against an Armed Forces team that included future Hall-of-Famer Joe DiMaggio. When DiMaggio clouted a homer, Max went crazy. He threw his glove down in disgust and stomped around the mound. Next, he twisted his cap so the brim faced sideways and contorted his face into wild expressions. As DiMaggio

rounded the bases, Max Patkin took off after him. He followed Joe all the way home as the crowd laughed and applauded. And that's how Max Patkin's baseball clown act was born.

HEROIC FEET

Frank "Ping" Bodie was best known as the lonely roommate of New York Yankees star Babe Ruth. Babe spent so many nights out on the town that Ping once commented he "roomed with Babe Ruth's suitcase."

During a game in 1917, Bodie was thrown out by a wide margin while trying to steal a base. This prompted sports reporter Art Baer to write, "His heart was full of larceny, but his feet were honest."

NUTS AND BOLTS

In 1996, Chicago Cubs reliever Bob Patterson delivered up a game-winning home pitch to Cincinnati Reds' batter Barry Larkin. When asked about the pitch, Patterson quipped, "It was a cross between a screwball and a change-up . . . a screw-up."

HO-HUM

Johnny Logan, who played shortstop for the Milwaukee Braves in the early 1950s, never failed to amuse anyone who listened to him butcher the English language. A reporter once asked why the Braves were in a slump. "We're just tiresome, that's all," Johnny Logan explained.

On another occasion, a teammate introduced Logan to a friend who was visiting. Johnny stared at the visitor and muttered, "I know the name, but I can't replace the face."

INDEX

ABOUT THE AUTHOR

Michael Morgan Pellowski lives with a family of athletes. Michael went to Rutgers College on a football scholarship and won seven letters in football and baseball. In baseball, he posted a .314 career average. He was defensive captain of the football team and won A.P. and E.C.A.C. All-East honors. He also had pro football tryouts in the NFL and CFL.

Michael's wife, Judy, ran cross country and track in college. Their son Morgan won five letters in soccer, cross country and track, and was a cross country co-captain. He also played baseball and basketball. Son Matthew plays football, baseball, and basketball, and also ran cross country. Daughter Melanie plays softball and basketball, runs cross country, and is a cheerleader. Son Martin plays soccer, basketball, and baseball.